good MOUSEKEEPING

FOR DAVID, VERETTA, KAREN, ZACH, AND QUOTAS.

—JPL

FOR ME AND MY SISTER NATALIE.

—LD

Atheneum Books for Young Readers
An imprint of Simon & Schuster
Children's Publishing Division
1230 Avenue of the Americas
New York, New York 10020
Text copyright © 2001 by J. Patrick Lewis
Illustrations copyright © 2001 by Lisa Desimini
Book design by Angela Carlino
The text of this book is set in Helvetica Rounded Bold.
The illustrations are rendered in mixed media.
Printed in Hong Kong
1 2 3 4 5 6 7 8 9 10

Library of Congress Cataloging-in-Publication Data
Lewis, J. Patrick.
Good mousekeeping : and other animal home poems /
by J. Patrick Lewis ; illustrated by Lisa Desimini. — 1st ed.
p.   cm.
"An Anne Schwartz book."
Summary: A collection of humorous poems that describe
where various animals would reside, if they could decide.
ISBN 0-689-83161-7
1. Animals—Juvenile poetry. 2. Children's poetry, American.
[1. Animals—Poetry. 2. American poetry.]
I. Desimini, Lisa, ill. II. Title.
PS3562.E9465 G66 2002
811'.54—dc21   99-088259

FIRST
EDITION

good MOUSEKEEPING

and other animal home poems

AN ANNE SCHWARTZ BOOK

Atheneum Books for Young Readers

New York • London • Toronto • Sydney • Singapore

Do you suppose anyone knows
If animals like to spend
Their lives in hives and dingy dives?
"What would you recommend

In place of holes and Goldfish bowls,
Dark caves and distant trees?"
I asked a Bird, a Frog, a herd
Of Hippos. "Tell me, please,

Where would you stay . . . just for a day?"
I telephoned Giraffe.
He wasn't there—I called a Bear
And asked on his behalf.

And each one said, "A comfortable bed
That's certainly not in a cage!
We'd live on a street with all of the
Creature comforts. Turn the page!"

Oh, where would a Flamingo go?
She'd go to a Flamingolow,
A flaming hot pink bungalow
Beside the steamy jungle-o.

Houses meant for Porcupines
Always carry "Warning!" signs.

The Dragon's home
Has warmth and charm,
Four sprinklers and a
SMOKE ALARM!

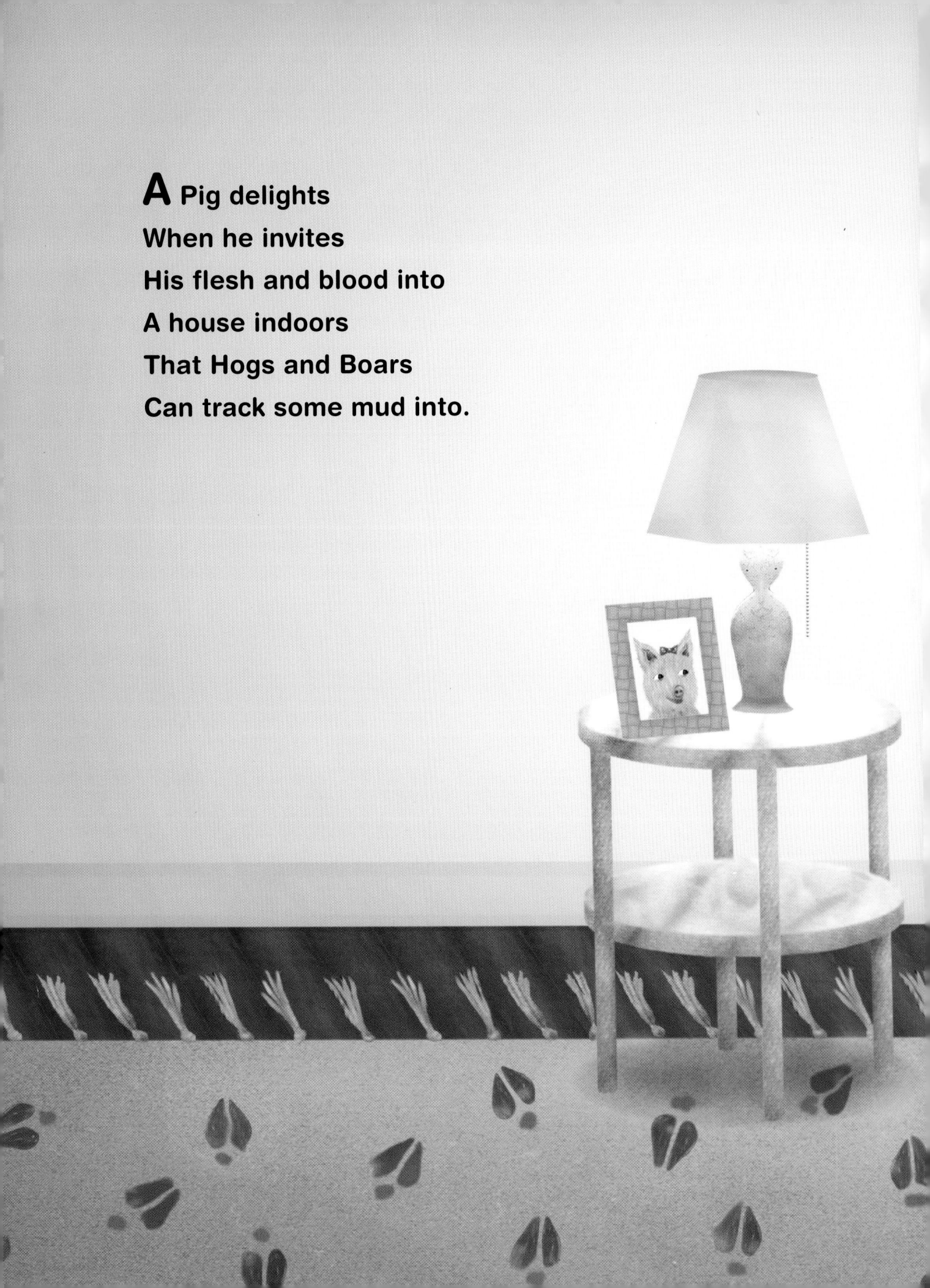

A Pig delights
When he invites
His flesh and blood into
A house indoors
That Hogs and Boars
Can track some mud into.

Chameleon's a shadow no one knows
And where he'd live is anybody's guess.
He'd camouflage like wallpaper to pose
But never leave a forwarding address.

The house a Skunk would call a home a-
Rises through a thick aroma.

Houses that please country Cats
Have furry *Welcome All Mice* mats
And front yards with ceramic rats.

One Cat loves buttermilk, but he's
Also fond of swiss and bries—
He calls his house . . .
THE COTTAGE CHEESE.

The Termite would
love any wood-
en neighborhood
that tasted good.

Cowbird's paradise?

Branch.

Ranch.

One gigantic love nest
With tons of hugs and kisses—
For the Hippopotamr.
And the Hippopotamrs.

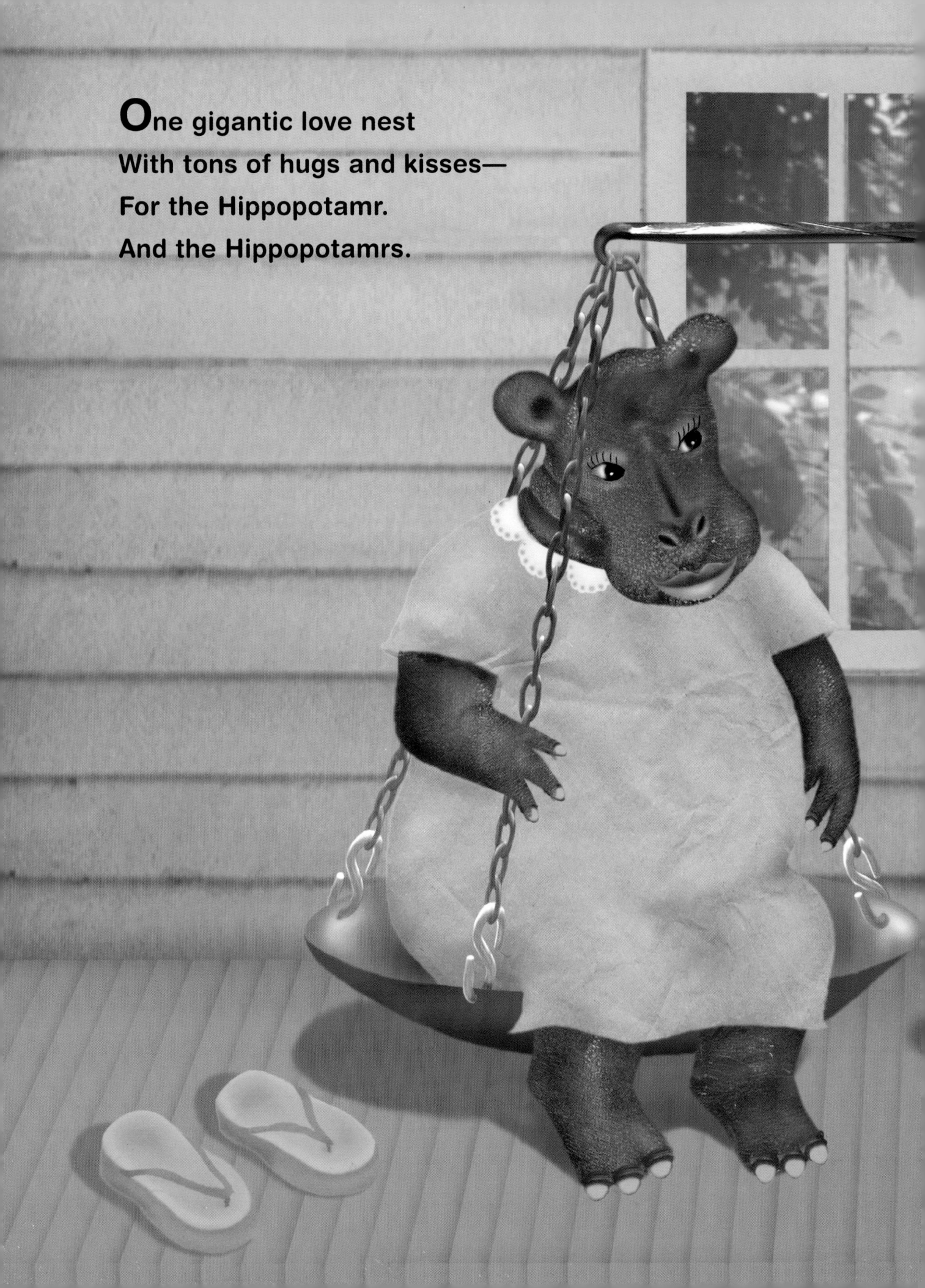

A house would make
A Bullfrog hopping mad
If it did not come with
A launching pad.

A house that suits a Polar Bear
Has very, very central air.

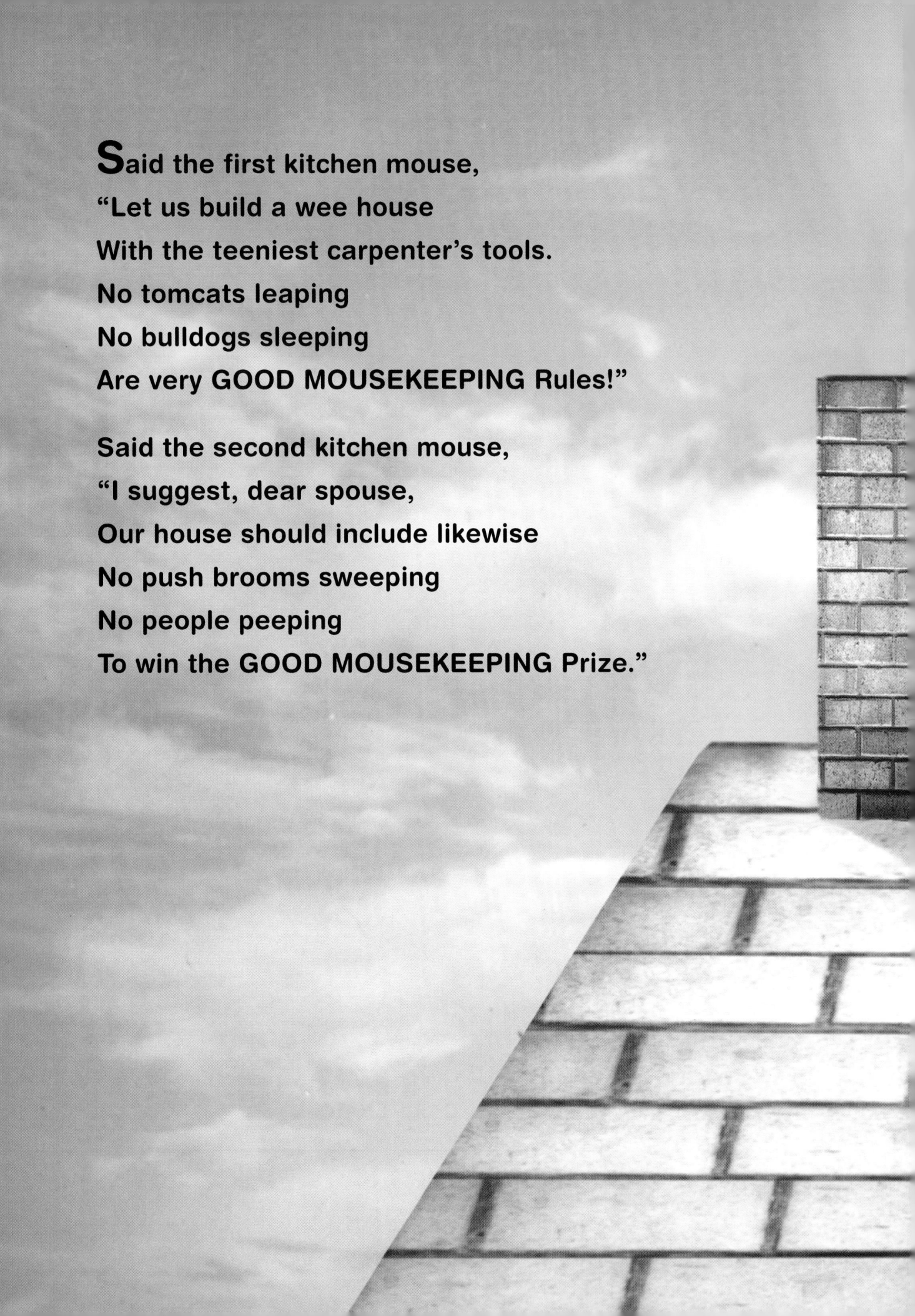

Said the first kitchen mouse,
"Let us build a wee house
With the teeniest carpenter's tools.
No tomcats leaping
No bulldogs sleeping
Are very GOOD MOUSEKEEPING Rules!"

Said the second kitchen mouse,
"I suggest, dear spouse,
Our house should include likewise
No push brooms sweeping
No people peeping
To win the GOOD MOUSEKEEPING Prize."

"**H**ere's what to do: Read slowly, chew
Delicious books, all ages,"
The Bookworm said, "but make your bed
With sheets of picture pages.

"Where would I rest? I'd get undressed
In Lewis Carroll's *Alice*
In Wonderland—a Cheshire Bookworm's
Curiouser word palace."

Garden apartment?
A Rabbit's digs
With tomato shingles,
Walls of twigs,
A carrot sidewalk.
Hedge? Swiss chard.
And broccoli trees—
In a raisin yard.

Higgledy-piggledy
House of a Porpoise is
Bobbing impossibly
Close to the shore!

Perfectly porpoisely,
Porpoises purposely
Surf through the windows and
Leap through the door.

A Turtle likes a humble home
To match his geodesic dome.

So Termite would chew on a rickety house,
And Dragon he says to me,
"I'm furnace, I'm oven, I'm chimney—I'm lovin'
The heat and humidity!"

Chameleon would crawl in a trickety house,
And Porpoise he says to me,
"What comfort I've found is a houseboat bound
Around the booming sea."

Porcupine pines for a prickety house,
And Polar Bear says to me,
"The weather's divine when the sun doesn't shine—
No home should be frost-free."

Pig would reside in a brickety house,
And Bookworm he says to me,
"I'm tastefully eating the book that you're reading!
A house that's a book
With a breakfast nook
Is house enough for me.
It's more than enough for me."

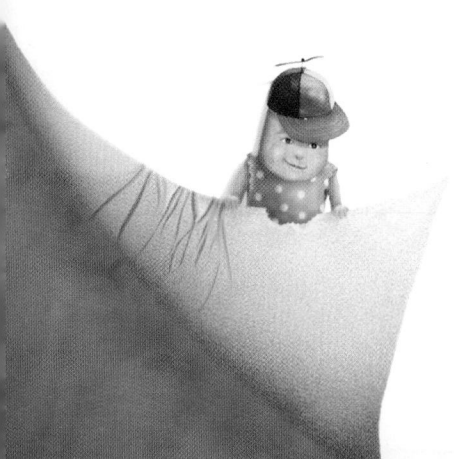

J. PATRICK LEWIS is one of the most respected children's poets in the United States. Among his many acclaimed titles are *The Boat of Many Rooms*; *A Hippopotamusn't,* which *Publishers Weekly* called "joyful exuberance . . . reminiscent of Ogden Nash"; and *Doodle Dandies: Poems That Take Shape.* He lives in Chagrin Falls, Ohio.

Good Mousekeeping grew out of an idea Lisa Desimini had while on tour with Mr. Lewis promoting *Doodle Dandies.* Inspired by her notion of houses animals might choose to live in, Mr. Lewis immediately imagined a polar bear choosing a house with very, *very* central air, and it became the first poem for the collection.

LISA DESIMINI is the illustrator of many books for children, including *Anansi Does the Impossible,* by Verna Aardema; *Doodle Dandies: Poems That Take Shape,* by J. Patrick Lewis; and *My House,* which was selected as a *New York Times* Best Illustrated Book. She also illustrated the jackets for several of Barbara Kingsolver's best-selling novels.

Ms. Desimini created the art for *Good Mousekeeping* by scanning into the computer drawings, paintings, fabrics, photos, and other materials such as: a big furry black hat (for the pig), a Popsicle stick (for the dragon's tail and tower), feathers (for the flamingo), velvet (for the pig's skirt and love seat), and a dish towel (for the polar bear). A graduate of the School of Visual Arts, she lives in New York City.